Copyright © Atsons Tra

All rights reserved. Without limiting the rig above, no part of this publication may be p introduced into a retrieval system or transmitted in any form or by any means (electronic, mechanical, photocopying or otherwise) without the prior written permission of the copyright owner and publisher of this Travel Guide.

We have relied on our own experience as well as many different sources for this Travel Guide, and we have done our best to check facts and to give credit where it is due. In the event that any material is incorrect or has been used without proper permission, please contact us so that the oversight can be corrected.

Cover photo by Roberto Taddeo / Flickr

Written by: Shea Robinson

Edited by: Bruno Luis

Contents

Introduction to Naples	3
#1 Pompeii	4
#2 Cappella Sansevero	6
#3 National Archaeological Museum of Naples	8
#4 San Gregorio Armeno	10
#5 Mount Vesuvius	12
#6 Bourbon Tunnel	14
#7 Teatro di San Carlo	16
#8 Castel dell'Ovo	18
#9 Spaccanapoli	20
#10 Catacombs of San Gennaro	22
#11 Santa Chiara	24
#12 Lungomare Caracciolo	26
#13 Gesù Nuovo	28
#14 Certosa di San Martino	30
#15 Museo di Capodimonte	32
#16 Naples Cathedral	34
#17 Fontanelle Cemetery	36
#18 Royal Palace of Naples	38
#19 Castel Nuovo	40
#20 Castel Sant'Elmo	42
Map of Attractions in Central Naples	44
Map of Attractions in Outer Naples	45

Introduction to Naples

Italy's third largest city and one of its oldest, Naples is stunningly situated on the Gulf of Naples and in the shadow of the dominating Mount Vesuvius. The irresistible charm of this wonderful city can be felt from the UNESCO World Heritage Site listed centro storico (historic centre) to the castles and palaces which line the waterfront.

Here is a place for the cultured, with some of Europe's finest museums and galleries, the historic, with incredible archaeological sites, and the culinary with restaurants serving up everything from traditional dishes to incredible fresh seafood dishes and sweet treats.

Naples proudly displays its diverse history from the National Archaeological Museum of Naples and the Pausilypon Archaeological Park through to its wonderful castles; Castel dell'Ovo, Castel Nuovo, and Castel dell'Elmo.

Discover the city's love affair with Baroque at Cappella Sansevero, Gesu Nuovo, Naples Cathedral, and the Royal Palace of Naples while admiring works by some of the greatest artists the country has produced at Museo di Capodimonte and Santa Chiara. Dive underground into the hidden past of the city at the Bourbon Tunnel, the Catacombs of San Gennaro, and the Fontanelle Cemetery.

Take in the sights with a stroll along Spaccanapoli or meander around the Gulf of Naples at Lungomare Caracciolo. Mount Vesuvius is never outside your peripheral vision and a trip to the dormant volcano is rewarded with incredible views of the city, Gulf, and countryside. Relax and enjoy the ride as you uncover Italy's improbable masterpiece.

#1 Pompeii

© Flickr / Glen Scarborough

Perhaps the most famous of all ancient Roman towns, Pompeii's desolate streets provide a bleak reminder of the power contained within Mount Vesuvius. Listed as a UNESCO World Heritage Site, the ancient town has been one of Europe's most popular tourist attractions for over 250 years.

Before the eruption of Vesuvius in 79 AD, Pompeii was a thriving commercial centre and boasted a population of approximately 11,000 people. It is believed the town was founded in the 7th or 6th Century BC by the Osci on an important trade crossroads. During the 6th and 5th Centuries BC, the town was captured by the Greek colony of Cumae and later by the Samnites before becoming a Roman colony in the 1st Century BC by the name of 'Colonia Cornelia Veneria Pompeinorum'.

As a Roman colony, the town thrived and excavations have

revealed a complex water system, a gymnasium, a port, and an amphitheatre among other buildings and features associated with a Roman town. The unique preservation of the town also shows details of everyday life at this time such as wine jars, graffiti, frescoes, and details of individual professions.

At the time of the eruption, the town had become a popular holiday destination and may have had up to 20,000 inhabitants. On August 24th in 79 AD, Mount Vesuvius erupted with first-hand accounts recorded by Pliny the Younger from a position across the Bay of Naples. Hot surges from the volcano at around 250 degrees Celsius would have caused instant death to many in the town with 12 layers of ash raining down for six hours suffocating the rest.

Pompeii remained buried for centuries, until excavations in 1748 by Rocque Joaquin de Alcubierre. Numerous excavations continued over the following decades, revealing more intimate details of the people who inhabited the town at the time of the eruption

Today, the remains form part of the larger Vesuvius National Park which incorporates the nearby town of Herculaneum and Stabiae, both of which were also buried under ash from Vesuvius.

The Streets of Pompeii

It is highly recommended to get a map from the ticket office as there are numerous buildings and attractions to be found throughout the town with the highlights including the amphitheatre, the gymnasium, the forum, and the baths.

Combining a visit to Pompeii with a trip to the National Archaeological Museum in Naples is highly recommended as it is where the best preserved items and mosaics from the town are kept.

#2 Cappella Sansevero

© Flickr / David Sivyer

Officially named the Chapel of Santa Maria della Pieta, Cappella Sansevero houses numerous masterpieces and artistic wonders from the 18th Century. Originally built in 1590 as the funerary chapel of the di Sangro family, it was given its Baroque style makeover in the mid-18th Century by the eccentric prince of Sansevero, Raimondo di Sangro.

The prince hired the most impressive sculptors of the day to perform the decoration, some of which included Masonic symbolism, and commissioned the finest artists of the day to lavish the interior. The chapel's official name came from a painting of the Virgin Mary (La Pieta) which was spotted in the chapel in 1623, leading to it originally being dedicated to Santa Maria della Pieta upon completion of the construction.

Inside, the Cappella Sansevero consists of a rectangular nave surrounded by eight moderate chapels, with two doors in the centre leading into the crypt. In stark contrast to the modest exterior of the building, the interior is richly decorated with sculptures, frescoes, marble, and mosaics. The ceiling was painted by Francesco Maria Russo in 1749 in a series of frescoes which have been untouched since their creation.

The frescoes are said to have maintained their bright colours due to a solution created by Russo which replaced the glue which was usually found in the frescoes of the time. The original floor was a giant black and white mosaic which represented the Masonic symbol of a labyrinth, although most of the original floor was replaced in 1901 after a collapse of the chapel 12 years previous.

Among the most interesting sculptures is Francesco Queirolo's Disinganno, showing a man attempting to free himself from a net, symbolic of the freedom from earthly deceit. The man attempting to untangle himself is Riamondo's father, Antonio, who abandoned the young prince to travel and enjoy hedonistic pleasures. Becoming repentant in his later years, Antonio returned to Naples and attempted to free himself from sin by joining the priesthood.

© Wikimedia / Liberonapoli

The Veiled Christ

The true masterpiece of the Cappella, however, is the Veiled Christ by Giuseppe Sanmartino. Created in 1753, it is considered to be among the greatest masterpieces in the world, displaying such incredible detail that one is tempted to attempt lifting the veil to view Christ underneath.

In the crypt, two perfectly preserved human arterial systems are on display, both of which remain the subject of debate as to whether they are real or reproductions.

7

#3 National Archaeological Museum of Naples

© Flickr / Nick Bramhall

Italy's most impressive archaeology museum and one of the most important museums of its kind in the world, the National Archaeological Museum of Naples (or MANN as it is known locally) is situated at the corner of the original Greek wall of the city Neapolis and houses a substantial collection of artefacts from Herculaneum, Stabiae, and Pompeii.

Founded by Charles III of Spain in the 1750s, the building acted as a cavalry barracks and as the seat of the University of Naples for over 150 years until it became home to a vast collection of Greek and Roman antiquities including gems, coins, gold and silver, mosaics, and Roman erotica discovered at Pompeii.

The basement of the museum is home to a variety of Egyptian relics and epigraphs from the Borgia collection, while the ground level concentrates on colossal Roman and Greek sculptures from the Farnese collection.

Highlights here include the Toro Farnese (Farnese Bull) which was sculpted in the 3rd Century and thought to be a Roman copy of a Greek statue which depicts the death of the Queen of Thebes and was restored by the great Michelangelo, and the Ercole (Hercules) which was originally uncovered without his legs until they showed up in a later excavation and were re-attached.

On the mezzanine level, the display consists of an extraordinary collection of mosaics found mainly at Pompeii including a depiction of Alexander the Great.

Moving beyond the collection of mosaics, the Gabinetto Segreto (Secret Chamber) is home to a small collection of ancient erotica. These much-studied pieces include a series of nine paintings which display various erotic positions, thought to be a sort of menu for ancient brothels.

© Wikimedia / Marie-Lan Nguyen

The Toro Farnese

The first floor is home to a series of incredible discoveries from Cuma, Pompeii, Boscoreale, Stabaie, and Herculaneum alongside the Farnese Atlante, a statue of Atlas carrying a globe.

When entering the museum, be sure to pick up an invaluable audio guide which will not only help you navigate the museum, but also provide some fascinating backstories to many of the objects.

#4 San Gregorio Armeno

© Wikimedia / Armando Mancini

One of the most important Baroque complexes in Naples, the San Gregorio Armeno complex knows no bounds in its rich ornamentation. The complex was constructed in the 10th Century, on the remains of a Roman temple which was dedicated to Ceres, by a group of nuns fleeing the Byzantine Empire with precious relics of St. Gregory, the Bishop of Armenia.

It was he who the monastic complex was named after, although his relics weren't all the nuns carried with them. They also carried the dried blood and relics of St. Patrizia, who died in Naples sometime between the 4th and 8th Centuries upon felling Constantinople. The powdered vials of blood are said to liquefy every Tuesday, unlike those of Saint Gennaro whose blood only liquefies twice a year.

Accessible via a gate are the complex's incredible cloisters. Peaceful, they feature an eccentric fountain decorated with sea horses, dolphins, and masks alongside two sublime statues portraying Christ and Samaritan.

On the southern side of the cloisters is the old bakery of the convent which still contains many of the cooking utensils used by the nuns.

Beside the bakery is the Cappella dell'Idria which is the only surviving section of the original medieval convent. Inside, wonderful Baroque paintings portraying the Life of Mary by Paolo De Matteis adorn the walls. Above the high alter is the icon of Madonna dell'Idria in beautiful Byzantine style.

Moving on from the cloisters, it is possible to enter the stunningly decorated coro delle monache (nuns' choir stall) which peer down onto the church's altar and nave.

If you are lucky in the timing of your visit you may catch a peek of the wooden nativity scene which dates back over 600 years, although it is generally kept hidden away in a cabinet.

© Wikimedia / Armando Mancini

The Cappella dell'Idria

The discreet windows which can be seen lining the cupola above the choir stall belong to a second choir stall used by bed-ridden nuns so they could attend mass.

Other highlights found throughout the complex include Luca Giordano's fresco 'The Embarkation, Journey and Arrival of the Armenia Nuns with the Relics of Saint Gregory', and the superb altar by Dionisio Lazzari.

#5 Mount Vesuvius

© Flickr / CucombreLibre

Towering over the Gulf of Naples, Mount Vesuvius is shrouded in history, myth, and legend. Since famously blowing its top in 79AD, leading to the destruction of Herculaneum and Pompeii, the volcano has erupted a further 30 times, most devastatingly in 1631 and even as recently as 1944. In fact, Mount Vesuvius has lost over 800 metres in height due to the violet outburst which occurred in 79AD and subsequent explosions, standing at 1281 metres today.

The devastating effects of its most famous explosion not only created a giant crater and two new peaks on the mountain but also pushed the coastline back several kilometres, spewed debris to a height of 33 kilometres, and released energy equivalent to that of one hundred thousand times of the energy released by the Hiroshima bombing.

Today, the volcano is considered the most dangerous in the world due to its geographical location, where it is in close proximity to a population of over 3 million people, making it the most populated volcanic region in the world.

However, it is also a once in a lifetime experience to observe the wonderful panorama gained from the crater of the currently dormant volcano.

Free guided tours include a walk around the crater from where breath-taking views of the Apennine Mountains, islands dotted around Gulf of Naples, the city of Naples, Mount Picentini, and much more can be gained.

The climb to the summit from the carpark is a manageable 860 metres, where you will pass by the remains of a funicular which was opened in 1880 and destroyed by the last eruption in 1944. Be warned, it can become quite chilly even in the summer so ensure you are well prepared.

The surrounding area of Mount Vesuvius was proclaimed a national park in 1995, named after the volcano the area provides some wonderful walking trails around the iconic giant. When entering the national park, be sure to pick up a map of the trails from the information office, with walking times varying from a couple of hours to half a day.

© Wikimedia / Morn the Gorn

Mount Vesuvius as Seen from Pompeii

Also located in the vicinity of the volcano is the fascinating Museo dell'Osservatorio Vesuviano which displays details documented over two millennia by people who have kept a close watch over Vesuvius

13

#6 Bourbon Tunnel

© www.galleriaborbonica.com / Photo by Vittorio Sciosia

Used throughout history as an aqueduct, an escape passageway, an air raid shelter, and an impound lot, the Bourbon Tunnel brings visitors on a journey through half a century of Neapolitan history over 30 metres below the city.

The tunnel was conceived by King Ferdinand II of Bourbon, who wished to use it as a military passageway, which would connect Via Morelli with the Royal Palace of Naples, and as an escape route for its royal inhabitants should a repeat of the riots during the Revolt of Masaniello, from which he narrowly escaped to a nearby convent, occur.

The king commissioned Errico Alvino to construct the passageway underneath the streets of Naples by boring through the hill of Pizzofalcone through to the quartiere of San Ferdinando. He also used the Carmignano Aqueduct system which provided water to the inhabitants of the Monte di Dio district to connect the underground network of tunnels.

Only two years after construction of the tunnels began, the Bourbon dynasty fell and work was grounded to a halt. The incomplete tunnel complex was used during the Second World War as a shelter from the regular air raids and bombings which took place, and as a military hospital. During this time, the Bourbon Tunnel provided aid and shelter to over 100,000 inhabitants of Naples.

When the war had finished, the tunnels were used as an impound lot until the 1970s, when they were abandoned until five years of restoration work resulted in them re-opening as a tourist attraction in 2010.

Tours of the tunnels are truly fascinating, with vehicles from the early 20th Century, statues, and remnants from the Second World War visible throughout. There are three different kinds of tours available; the 'Standard Tour', the 'Adventure Tour', and the 'Speleo Tour'.

© www.galleriaborbonica.com / Photo by Vittorio Sciosia

An Abandoned Car Inside the Tunnel

The Standard Tour allows visitors to walk through the tunnel, in to the water tanks, and around the areas where the bomb shelters once stood. The Adventure Tour is more concentrated on the old Aqueduct system and includes a raft ride along an abandoned part of the tunnel which has become flooded by water.

The Speleo Tour offers a degree of freedom, providing guests with lights, helmets, and suits and allowing them to wander around the underground complex at their own leisure.

#7 Teatro di San Carlo

Once the largest opera house in the world, Teatro di San Carlo epitomises Italy's love and passion for the arts. Built in 1737, decades before the renowned Milanese La Scala and Venetian La Fenice, it is the oldest and most continuously active public opera house in Europe. Its construction was commissioned by Charles VII of Naples, a member of the Bourbon dynasty, who wanted to replace the dilapidated Teatro San Bartolomeo with a larger and more extravagant opera house.

The design was created by Giovanni Antonio Medrana and Angelo Carasale, and was to include a large hall measuring 28.6 metres by 22.5 metres, 184 boxes along with a royal box, gold decoration, blue upholstery, and exquisite architecture. In total, the new opera house could hold an audience of over 3,000 with 1,379 seated and the remaining standing, cost 75,000 ducats to build, and was the largest in the world at the time.

On November 4th 1737, the Teatro di San Carlo was inaugurated with a performance of Domenico Darro's 'Achille in Sirco', an opera based on the libretto by Metastasio and had been set to music by Antonio Caldara.

Numerous illustrious names brought performances to the San Carlo over the years including Christoph Willbald Gluck's 'Clemenza di Tito' and Johann Christian Bach's 'Catone in Utica' and 'Alessandro nell'Indie'.

In 1816, the opera house was destroyed by a fire which broke out during a dress-rehersal, but was quickly reconstructed by order of King Ferdinand IV, another Bourbon monarch. The architect, Antonio Niccolini, who was commissioned to reconstruct the building created a more traditional horse-shoe style auditorium and completed the job within ten months.

Today, access to the San Carlo can be gained by guided tour or attending a performance. There is room for around 1,500 spectators in the auditorium, however, tickets can sell out quickly so if you are planning to attend a performance be sure to book in advance. The interior of the building is lavishly decorated with gold and red and contains a stunning fresco by Guiseppe Cammarano on the ceiling which represents the Goddess Minerva and the Greek God Apollo.

© Wikimedia / Viva-Verdi

Exterior of the Opera house

During the guided tour, you will be brought through the main theatre hall, the Royal box, the main boxes, and the two Foyers, with entrance to the Multimedia Museum of Teatro di San Carlo (MeMUS) also available for an extra fee.

17

#8 Castel dell'Ovo

© Flickr / Lukemn

The oldest castle in Naples, Castel dell'Ovo (translated as Egg Castle) pokes out into the Gulf of Naples on the former tiny island of Megaride, now a peninsula. It was this island where Siren Partenope washed ashore after throwing herself into the sea due to a failed attempt in luring Ulysses and provided Naples with its first name, Pertenope.

However, it was the legend written by the infamous Roman poet Virgil which provided the castle with its name. According to myth, Virgil placed an egg in a glass jar, and the jar in a metal cage which he hid beneath the castle. As long as the egg remained untouched and intact, the city would survive.

The only flaw with this myth is that around the time Virgil was alive (70BC – 19BC), Castel dell'Ovo wasn't actually a castle but an expansive villa by the name of Castellum Lucullanmum.

It wasn't until the 12th Century that Castel dell'Ovo was constructed under the Normans and made seat of the conquered city of Naples in 1140 by the Roger the Norman.

Its importance declined somewhat upon the construction of Castel Nuovo under Charles I of Anjou, but it remained the seat of the Royal Chamber and State Treasury as well as serving as the city prison.

Numerous rulers added their touches to the castle over the following centuries, with none more evident than that by the Aragonese domination. Its guns were used by rebels in the Neapolitan Republic of 1799 and it continued to be used as a prison until the 19th Century when a small fishing village named Borgo Marinaro developed around the eastern wall.

Today, the small village has provided a marina and numerous restaurants around the castle which have become part of the allure. The structure of the castle is rectangular with a high bastion which rewards visitors with breath-taking panoramas of the surrounding area.

© Wikimedia / Producer

Castel dell'Ovo

The 100 metre causeway has become a popular location for wedding photos due to the postcard-like background combination of the marina and castle.

Inside, the prison cells which were part of the castle for over seven centuries are long gone and the main halls play host to a variety of art exhibitions, local events, and wine trade shows and fairs.

#9 Spaccanapoli

© Wikimedia / Velvet

Following the path of the ancient Roman decumanus inferior (minor road) and the most southern of the three decumani (east-west streets) which formed the grid of the Greco-Roman city of Neapolis, Spaccanapoli (Break Naples) is affectionately called so due to the fact that from above it seems to cut through the heart of the city.

The street is officially called Via Benedetto Croce, becoming Via Benedetto Croce to the west and Via Vicaria Vecchia to the east, and passes numerous important sights along the way, making it a tourist highway for sightseeing.

Starting at the eastern end of Spaccanapoli, the Ospedale delle Bambole is a shop which contains assorted mannequins and dolls heads which has become a sort of local institution.

Moving along the street, the Chiesa di Sant'Angelo a Nilo is a modest 14th Century church which is presided over by four pot-bellied gilt cherubs. Inside the church, one can find the magnificent Renaissance tomb of Cardinal Brancaccio which was sculpted by the great Donatello among others.

On the popular Piazza Domenico Maggiore stands the Gothic Chiesa di San Domenico Maggiore which was a favourite of Angevin nobility upon its completion in the early 12th Century.

The combination of 19th Century Neo-Gothic and Baroque styles inside complement each other wonderfully, while fine 14th Century frescoes by Pietro Cavallini and 45 coffins of nobles including Aragon princes make this church a must-see.

Nearby, the simple façade of the Cappella Sansevero is in stark contrast to the incredible sculptures which lay inside. Highlights here include the Veiled Christ by Giuseppe Sanmartino and the perfectly preserved human arterial systems in the basement.

Beyond the churches, there are numerous shopping opportunities from high-street stores to chic fashion boutiques and market stalls selling almost everything you can imagine, while charming cafés and coffee shops make the perfect place to relax for a spot of lunch.

© Flickr / Roberto Taddeo

Spaccanapoli Seen from Castel Sant'Elmo

Keep an eye out for side streets such as Via San Gregorio Armeno where traditional presepio (nativity scene) figurine making is still practised. The tourist office faces the square on Piazza Gesu Nuovo, where you can pick up a map with various walking routes along Spaccanapoli.

#10 Catacombs of San Gennaro

© Flickr / Rosino

The largest complex of its kind in Southern Italy, the Catacombs of San Gennaro are an elaborate network of chapels, ambulatories, tunnels, and cubicles. Spread over three underground levels, this burial chamber is found below the volcanic rock of Capodimonte Hill. Originally, however, they were three separate cemeteries dedicated to Saint Gaudiosus, Saint Severus, and Saint Januarius and differed from other similar Roman burial sites due to the spacious passageways along two of the levels.

The deepest level is the oldest of three, dating back to the 3rd Century and could possibly have even been the burial site of a much earlier, pre-Christian sect. During this time, the catacombs were the burial place for numerous Roman noblemen and the first patron saint of Naples, Sant'Agrippino, although his remains were later moved.

After the burial of Sant'Agrippino, the lands became an important religious burial site, leading to the expansion of the second level in order to encompass the other two levels.

In the 5th Century, the remains of San Gennaro, another patron saint of Naples, were moved here and although he was moved again to Benevento in the 10th Century and to a crypt beneath Naples Cathedral in the 15th Century, his tomb which contains the oldest known portrait of him is still visible today.

Another point of interest inside the catacombs is the tiny Basilica of Sant'Agrippino, which remains in use today and is decorated with ceiling frescoes dating between the 2nd and 10th Centuries alongside more contemporary art works.

When exploring the catacombs, it becomes obvious that social class played a part in the type of tomb one was buried in. The wealthy buried here generally opted for an open-room cubiculum which would've been guarded by gates and most likely adorned with thrilling frescoes, although many have faded or disappeared over time.

© Wikimedia / AlMare

Fresco in the Catacombs of San Gennaro

One fresco which remains intact can be found near the entrance and features a mother, father, and child which is in fact three separate layers of frescoes commissioned for each death.

The smaller wall niches, known as loculum, were taken by normal middle-class people, while the floor tombs (forme) were where the poor were buried. A tour of the catacombs finishes at the Basilica of San Gennaro dei Poveri, where you may continue on to the Catacombs of San Gaudioso if you wish.

#11 Santa Chiara

© Wikimedia / IlSistemone

Consisting of the Church of Santa Chiara, an archaeological museum, a monastery, and numerous tombs, Santa Chiara is a stunning religious complex and a rare example of the city's Gothic history. The complex was built by Queen Sancha of Majorca and King Robert of Naples in the 12th Century in a traditional Gothic design, however, it was redecorated in a Baroque style by Domenico Antonio Vaccaro in the 17th Century.

The edifice of the complex was almost completely destroyed during the Second World War, leading to a re-construction in which an attempt was made to restore its original state. The ten-year long renovation was subject to some controversy, but upon completion in 1953 many agreed that the complex had returned to its original Gothic splendour. When it was re-opened, the first chapel on the left of the entrance was dedicated to national hero,

Salvo D'Acquisto, who sacrificed his life during the war so that 22 others could live.

The architecture of the Santa Chiara has a number of unusual features such as the lack of an apse and how the lateral chapels are absorbed into the body of the church, producing a very distinctive rectangular shape. Behind the main alter, the tomb of King Robert can be found with a wall separating the body of the church from the nuns' choir behind that.

Numerous other tombs are contained within the side chapels including that of Francis II, his consort Maria Sophie of Bavaria, Queen Maria Christina of Savoy, and the national hero Salvo D'Acquisto. The stuccoed ceiling is a result of the Baroque refurbishment of the complex in the 18th Century and was frescoed by artists such as Paolo de Maio, Guiseppe Bonito, and Francesco De Mura.

Also contained within the complex of Santa Chiara is the Majolica cloister which was transformed in the 18th Century with the addition of majolica tiles in a Rococo style, along with numerous murals and frescoes.

© Wikimedia / MatthiasKabel

The Majolica Cloister

From here you can easily reach the Museum of the Works or the Opera Museum, which houses a range of objects including documents, drawings, and pictures from the restoration of Santa Chiara, along with a collection of pottery, reliquaries, sculpture, and decorative arts which survived the bombings in World War II and cover the history of Naples.

Also, take some time to visit the archaeological area contained within the complex which was discovered after the war. Here, you can find a Roman thermal bath complex similar to those of Heroulancum or Pompeii.

2 Lungomare Caracciolo

A stunning pedestrianized promenade stretching almost three kilometres around the Gulf of Naples, Lungomare Caracciolo is an oasis from the city with some of the most breath-taking panorama views in Europe. The area which stretches from Mergellina to the west and Via Partenope on the east was only occasionally closed to traffic on Sundays until the seafront was chosen as the host location for the America's Cup in 2012.

Since then, strong backing from the city's mayor has seen the area remain car free, leading to it becoming an epicentre for outdoor events and sporting activity.

Strolling along the promenade you are likely to see locals and tourists mixing in tennis matches, basketball tournaments, kite flying, beach volleyball, or playing a game of beach soccer while crowds gather to watch on the JumboTron. If sports aren't for you, it is possible to rent a bicycle or pair of rollerblades to wiz along the seafront or simply top up your tan while relaxing to the sound of the waves.

Lungomore Caracciolo also passes numerous points of interest beginning with Castel dell'Ovo which pokes out into the Gulf to the east and is surrounded by the tiny village of Borgo Marinari, famous for its restaurants and cafés.

Dominating the landscape behind the castle is Mount Vesuvius which blends into the Sorrentine Peninsula providing a once-in-a-lifetime photo opportunity.

Sitting in the middle of the Gulf is the distinct shape of Capri which points towards Posillipo and Mergellina to the west of the promenade. Turn your back on the Gulf to see the outline of the city climbing up Naples hills with the San Martino Chaterhouse and Castel Sant'Elmo looking down from the summit.

Along the seafront, white rocks and small enclosures of sand offer the perfect place to take the sun while the more adventurous can rent a boat and explore the Gulf. Restaurants and cafés along Via Partonope offer al tresco dining, serving fresh seafood and traditional pizza with a side of perfect views of the bay.

© Wikimedia / Johnnyrotten

Lungomare Caracciolo

Keep an eye out for restaurants which offer free bike rental to their diners and take a ride to Europe's oldest aquarium, the Naples Aquarium, after a spot of lunch. At sunset, grab a gelato and take a seat along the seawall for one of the most romantic views in the city.

#13 Gesù Nuovo

© Flickr / mweav31

Standing in a piazza of the same name, Gesu Nuovo (Jesus Church) is the city's finest example of Renaissance architecture. Originally built as a palace for Prince Roberto Sanseverino of Salerno in the 15th Century, a church built by the Jesuits by the name of Gesu Nuovo already existed in Naples at the time.

By the mid-16th Century, the Sanseverino family had fallen out of favour due to political intrigues, and the property was confiscated and sold to the Jesuits for a price of 45,000 ducats.

The Jesuits hired architect Guiseppe Valeriano to convert the building into a church which began in 1584. The decision was made to maintain the unusual façade, originally intended for the palace, which consisted of rustic ashlar diamond projections. In the mid-18th Century, the Jesuits were expelled from Naples leaving the church to pass into the hands of the Franciscan order.

The unique façade of the church, covered in mini-pyramid shapes which in turn contain different symbols, was the subject of many conspiracy theories throughout the centuries until a few years ago when art historian Vincenzo De Pasquale recognised them as Aramaic letters which correspond to musical notes.

Inside, there are numerous frescoes, sculptures, and other masterpieces of art. At the back of the façade is a Baroque fresco by Francesco Solimena entitled 'The Expulsion of Heliodorus from the Temple', with the four pillars supporting the dome of the building containing frescoes of the four Evangelists by Giovanni Lanfranco.

Above the altar are eight busts of saints who glorified the Eucharist completed by Gennaro Cali and Costantino Labarbera.

Of the side chapels, the Chapel of the Visitation houses a bronze urn which contains the mortal remains of St. Joseph Moscati who was canonized by Pope John Paul II in 1987 along with a bronze statue of the saint to the left of the alter. The Chapel of Saint Francis Xavier contains three paintings by Luca Giordano and vault frescoes by De Matteis and Corenzio displaying episodes from the saint's life.

© Wikimedia / MIchel Rodriguez

Interior of the Church

The Sacred Heart Chapel has an altar-piece which was created by Giovanni Bernardino Azzolino in the 16th Century, the Chapel of St Ignatius of Loyola houses statues of Jeremiah and David by Cosimo Fanzago, and the Chapel of the Crucifix has a wooden statue sculpted by Francesco Mollica who was a pupil of Michelangelo.

#14 Certosa di San Martino

© Wikimedia / Armando Mancini

A former Christian monastery perched atop the Vomero hill, the Certosa di San Martino is now a museum which houses a number of Spanish and Bourbon artefacts alongside the finest displays of the presepe (Nativity scene) in the world. The history of the complex dates back to the 14th Century when it was inaugurated by the ruler of Naples, Queen Juan, as a monastery of the Carthusian order and dedicated to the medieval Christian Saint Martin.

Over the centuries, the complex underwent numerous renovations and expansions by some of the greatest Italian artists and architects, most significantly Giovanni Antonio Dosio in the 16th Century and Cosimo Fanzago in the 17th Century. The renovation designed by Fanzago provided the main shape, look, and feel of the monastery as it is today. In the 19th Century, the complex came under French rule and religious practise inside its walls was ceased.

Beginning in the monastery's church and rooms which flank it, one can observe an abundance of paintings and frescoes by the city's greatest 17th Century artists. The highlights here include works by Micco Spadaro, Massimo Stanzione, Francesco Solimena, Battista Caracciolo, Luca Giordano, and Giuseppe de Ribera, as well as the detail found in the sacristy.

Adjacent to the church is the smaller of the two cloisters, the Chiostro dei Procuratori, where a stately corridor on the left hand side leads to the Chiostro Grande (Great Cloister), considered to be among Italy's finest. Designed by Giovanni Antonio Dosio in the late 16th Century and expanded upon by Fanzago a century later, it is a superb combination of marble statues, porticoes, and garden ornamentation.

Just off the smaller cloister is the Sezione Navale, which focuses on the history of the Bourbon army in the 18th and 19th Centuries. Included in the exhibits are a series of scale models of warships, original naval weaponry, and a small collection of original royal barges. A true highlight in the museum is the Sezione Presepiale, displaying a rare collection of Neapolitan presepe ranging from the minuscule – a nativity scene in a decorated eggshell – to the enormous – a Cuciniello creation covering a whole wall of what used to be the kitchen.

© Wikimedia / Lalupa

Interior of the Church

In the southern wing, the Quarto del Priore is home to the majority of the picture collection including the museum's most famous piece, La vergine col bambino e San Giovannino (Madonna and Child with the Infant John the Baptist) by Pietro Bernini. Another section of the museum not to be missed is the Immagini e Napoli (Images and Memories of Naples) which tells a pictorial history of the city.

#15 Museo di Capodimonte

© Wikimedia / Mentnafunangann

Housed in the expansive Palazzo Reale di Capodimonte which sits in the grounds of an idyllic park overlooking Naples, the Museo di Capodimonte contains one of the city's finest art collections. The palace was originally intended as a hunting lodge for King Charles VII of Naples and Sicily, however, as construction began in 1738 the plans for the buildings became grander and grander, eventually resulting in a monumental palace which became home to an art collection in 1759.

During this time the palace acted as both a residence and a museum, opening a laboratory for the restoration of paintings in 1787. Upon the declaration of the Parthenopean Republic in 1799, French troops looted and occupied the palace with most of the artworks being transferred to the National Archaeological Museum of Naples.

After the Italian Reunification in 1861, the palace passed to the House of Savoy and numerous pieces were added to the collection. In 1950, the palace was given to the Italian state and became a national museum with many of the exhibits returning from the National Museum.

The Museo di Capodimonte is spread over three floors and 160 rooms, making it almost impossible to see the full collection in a single day. The first and second floors house the Galleria Nazionale (National Gallery) with paintings spanning the 13th to the 18th Centuries. Works by Botticelli, Titan, Masaccio, Bellini, and Caravaggio can be found on the first floor with numerous highlights including Bellini's Transfigurazione (Transfiguration), Masaccio's Crocifissione (Crucifixion), and Parmigianino's Antea.

The royal apartments are also located on the first floor, gloriously furnished with antique 18th Century furniture, a collection of majolica and porcelain from royal residences, and other excessive decoration. The most striking of these apartments is the Salottino di Porcellana which boasts wall-to-wall porcelain stucco.

© Wikimedia / Armando Mancini

One of the Rooms of the Museum

The second floor hosts a superb collection of paintings by Neapolitan artists alongside spectacular Belgian tapestries from the 16th Century. It is on this floor that the museum's most famous piece, Caravaggio's Flagellazione (Flagellation), is located in a room all to itself at the end of the corridor.

Also found on the second floor are a significant number of works from the Renaissance including paintings by Titan, Tintoretto, and Raphael. The third floor hosts a small contemporary gallery with the highlight being Andy Warhol's pop art painting Mt. Vesuvius.

#16 Naples Cathedral

© Flickr / Allan Parsons

The gleaming 19th Century Neo-Gothic façade of Naples Cathedral (called Il Duomo locally) is an understated beginning to the treasures which lie inside.

Originally commissioned by King Charles I of Anjou in 1272, construction continued under the rule of two subsequent monarchs – Charles II and Robert of Anjou – before it was consecrated in 1315. Built on the foundations of two palaeo-Christian basilicas, the remains of which can still be seen, excavations underneath the Cathedral have revealed numerous Roman and Greek artefacts.

An earthquake in 1456 destroyed much of the Cathedral, with numerous additions and expansions taking place in the subsequent centuries, the most recent being the addition of the façade in the 19th Century. Inside, the most famous part of the Cathedral is the Cappella di San

34

Gennaro (Chapel of St. Janurius) which was designed in 1637 by Giovanni Cola di Franco.

Many of the most celebrated artists of the time worked on the side chapel with highlights including an exciting canvas by Giuseppe de Ribera titled 'St Gennaro Escaping the Furnace Unscathed' and the incredible dome fresco by Giovanni Lanfranco.

Behind the altar, a strongbox contains the skull of San Gennaro and two phials of his blood. The phials of blood are brought out twice a year, on the first Saturday in May and on the 19th of September, when the dried blood liquefies.

It is said that if the blood fails to liquefy on these dates, disaster will befall the city of Naples. The next chapel to the east contains an urn with the saint's bones and below the high alter, Cappella Carafa houses even more of his remains.

Just off the north aisle of the Cathedral is one of the city's oldest basilicas, Basilica di Santa Restituta, which dates to the 4th Century, although it was subject to an extensive makeover after the earthquake in 1688.

Beyond this basilica is the fascinating archaeological zone which showcases the remains of Roman and Greek roads and buildings. It is here where you can also find the oldest baptistery in Western Europe containing wonderful 4th Century mosaics.

© Flickr / Francesco Sgroi

Interior of the Cathedral

Before you leave, be sure to head to the back of the left nave where a vault provides a glimpse into what the original Gothic structure of the Cathedral looked like before it was subject to a Baroque makeover.

35

#17 Fontanelle Cemetery

© Flickr / Antonio Manfredonio

Located in a cave in the Materdei hillside, it is estimated that Fontanelle Cemetery houses over eight million human bones. The cemetery is associated with folklore in the city, becoming a depository for every major epidemic Naples has suffered. In the 16th century, when the Spanish had moved into the city, there was major concerns over where cemeteries could be located and a decision was taken to move graves outside of the city walls.

However, many Neapolitans rejected this idea and insisted they were interred in their local churches.

To create space in the local churches, undertakers began removing the remains of the already deceased outside of the city walls to a cave located in the Materdei hillside, which became the Fontanelle Cemetery. At first, the remains which were taken to the cave were buried shallowly, however, the huge increase in bodies from the great plague of 1656 led to thousands being moved there.

According to the Neapolitan scholar, Andrea De Jorio, huge floods in the 17th Century washed many of the bones from the cave out into the streets of Naples. Due to this, the thousands of remains became anonymous and upon being returned, the cave became an unofficial burial place for the impoverished of the city. When Naples was under French rule in the early 19th Century, the cemetery officially became the resting place of the impoverished, with the last mass 'deposit' of bodies occurring in the wake of the cholera epidemic of 1837.

In 1872, Father Gaetano Barbati took it upon himself to organise and catalogue the chaotic skeletal remains in the cave and stored them on the surface in makeshift boxes and crypts. This gave rise to a cult of devotion to the remains of these anonymous people who prayed and paid respect to those who had been too poor to afford a proper burial. Members of the cult 'adopted' skulls, cleaned them, brought them flowers, and even talked to them.

The practise of the cult remained active for almost a century, even resulting in the construction of a small church at the entrance. However, in 1969, Cardinal Ursi of Naples decided that the devotion displayed by the cult had become a fetish and ordered the cemetery to shut down. Due to this, Fontanelle Cemetery suffered a long period of degradation, until a renovation project was started in 2002.

© Flickr / Fiore Silvestro Barbato

The Entrance to the Cemetery

In 2006, the cemetery reopened to the public for a few days each year. However, after protests in 2010, it was opened to the public full time. It is possible to visit the cemetery independently, but a lack of information in and around the site makes joining a guided tour much more rewarding.

#18 Royal Palace of Naples

© Wikimedia / Armando Mancini

Spanning the entire eastern end of Piazza del Plebiscito, the Royal Palace of Naples was one of four residences used by the Bourbon kings and is now home to the hugely impressive Royal House Museum. The palace was built on the site of an earlier residence, which was home to Don Pedro de Toledo, with construction of the current building beginning in the early 17th Century.

The palace was initially intended to host King Phillip III of Spain, although the king never arrived and instead it initially played host to Fernando Ruiz de Castro.

Construction and decoration of the palace was completed in 1644, and it remained the royal residence of the Austrians until the arrival of Charles III of Spain in 1734, when it became the royal residence of the Bourbons. During the time of the Bourbon reign, the palace was significantly damaged by a fire which led to major expansion and restoration in the mid-19th Century.

It was during these restorations that Francesco Antonio Picchiatti's Scalone d'onore, considered one of the finest staircases in Europe, was resurfaced in white and pink marble.

The staircase leads to the Museum of Palazzo Reale, also known as the Historic Apartment, which was opened to the public in 1919. Although it was damaged quite severely during World War II, the museum was beautifully restored and features a wonderful collection of Baroque and Neoclassical tapestries, paintings, furnishings, porcelain, decorative arts, and other objects.

Among the highlights are the Throne Room, Ferdinando Fuga's Court Theatre, a series of 12 paper mache statues dating from the 18th Century which survived the air raids during World War II and include Mercurio, Apollo, Minerva, and the nine muses. Another highlight can be found in the Royal Chapel, where a huge nativity scene featuring over 200 presepe figurines from the 18th and 19th Centuries can be found.

© Wikimedia / Armando Mancini

The Throne Room

The Royal Palace is also home to the National Library which was transferred here in 1925. Highlights in the library include papyrus scrolls uncovered at Herculaneum and the remains of a 5th Century Coptic bible.

Outside, the Giardino Romantico offers stunning views of Castel Nuovo and is home to a series of large stone horses erected above the San Carlo Theatre's practise room.

#19 Castel Nuovo

© Wikimedia / Sergio Parrella

Known locally as Maschio Angioino (Angevin Keep), Castel Nuovo's scenic location and commanding presence makes it one of Naples' most striking icons.

The history of the castle dates back to the 13th Century and Charles I of Naples (Charles of Anjou), who found himself in control of northern Italy, Tuscany, Provence, and the newly acquired southern Italy. Due to this, it made sense for him to make Naples his base and he commissioned an ambitious project to expand the city walls and port.

Part of his plans included converting the Franciscan convent into the castle which stands in Piazza Municipio today. The castle took three years to complete and was christened Castel Nuovo (New Castle) so it could be distinguished from the already existing Castel dell'Ovo and Castel Capuano.

Castel Nuovo quickly became the nucleus of the city under Charles II and played host to numerous important historical events such as the resignation of Pope Celestine V in 1294 and the election of Pope Boniface VIII 11 days later.

Under the rule of Robert the Wise, the castle was expanded and transformed into a centre of culture, playing host to the intellectual debates of the day. Such was its popularity that Giotto repaid his hosts by decorating much of the interior.

However, of the original structure only Cappella Palatina remains, as the rest of the castle is a result of the Aragonese renovations which took place in the 15th Century and heavy restoration works which were carried out prior to World War II.

The enormous Triumphal Arch which is erected between the Torre di Mezzo (Halfway Tower) and the Torre di Guardia (Watch Tower) commemorates Alfonso I of Aragon's victorious entry into the city in 1443, while the bleak Hall of the Barons is named after the slaughter which occurred here in 1486.

Inner Courtyard of the Castle

In Cappella Palatina, only small fragments of Giotto's frescoes remain while to the left of the chapel the Armoury Hall displays Roman ruins which were discovered here during restoration works.

This whole area forms part of the Municipal Museum which spreads over three floors and features a host of frescoes, sculptures, and paintings spanning the 14th to the 20th Centuries.

#20 Castel Sant'Elmo

© Flickr / János Korom Dr.

Perched atop Vomero Hill, the star-shaped Castel Sant'Elmo may be the baby of Naples' castles but it still forms an essential part of the city's skyline.

Originally a church dedicated to St. Erasmus, from which the castle's name is derived, the 12th Century fortress gained its distinct shape in the 16th Century under the designs of Pedro Luis Escriva, a military architect from Valencia.

For centuries, the castle was a symbol of government oppression, used to imprison Tommaso Campanella in 1604 and the patriots of the Neapolitan Revolution in 1799 including Mario Pagano, Luigia Sanfelice, and Gennaro Serra.

In fact, it remained a military prison right up until 1952 and a military property until 1976, when a huge renovation project was undertaken to recreate the original galleries, walkways, and underground chambers.

The major attraction for many at Castel Sant'Elmo are the jaw-dropping 360 degree panoramic views of the city, the bay, and Mount Vesuvius from the roof-top terrace which encircles the perimeter of the castle. The best time to visit is late afternoon, when views of the eastern side of the city are unimpeded and at their best.

One floor below the terrace, in the Piazza d'Armi, is the Napoli Novecento Museum. Opened in 2010, the museum is housed in the High Prison and displays an impressive collection of local art from the 20th Century including the Nuclear Art movement and Futurism.

Highlights include Eugenio Viti's La Schiena (The Back), Raffaele Lippi's Le Quattro Giornate di Napoli (The Four Days of Naples), and Salvatore Cotugno's sculpture of a wrapped and bound figure.

Back out in the Piazza d'Armi is Giancarlo Neri's enormous metal sculpture Luna e Laltra (the Mimmo Paladino helmet). Also housed within the castle is the Art History Library in the upper storey of the old prison block and a handful of administration offices including the Photographic Office and Thefts Office.

© Flickr / Roberto Taddeo

View of Naples from Castel Sant'Elmo

The castle has become part of the Neapolitan Museum Network and it is intended that in the near future, Castel Sant'Elmo will become the main centre for temporary and permanent exhibitions of contemporary art and performing arts in Naples.

Map of Attractions in Central Naples

#2 Cappella Sansevero

#3 National Archaeological Museum of Naples

#4 San Gregorio Armeno

#6 Bourbon Tunnel

#7 Teatro di San Carlo

#8 Castel dell'Ovo

#9 Spaccanapoli

#11 Santa Chiara

#12 Lungomare Caracciolo

#13 Gesù Nuovo

#14 Certosa di San Martino

#16 Naples Cathedral

#17 Fontanelle Cemetery

#18 Royal Palace of Naples

#19 Castel Nuovo

#20 Castel Sant'Elmo

Map of Attractions in Outer Naples

#1 Pompeii

#5 Mount Vesuvius

#10 Catacombs of San Gennaro

#15 Museo di Capodimonte

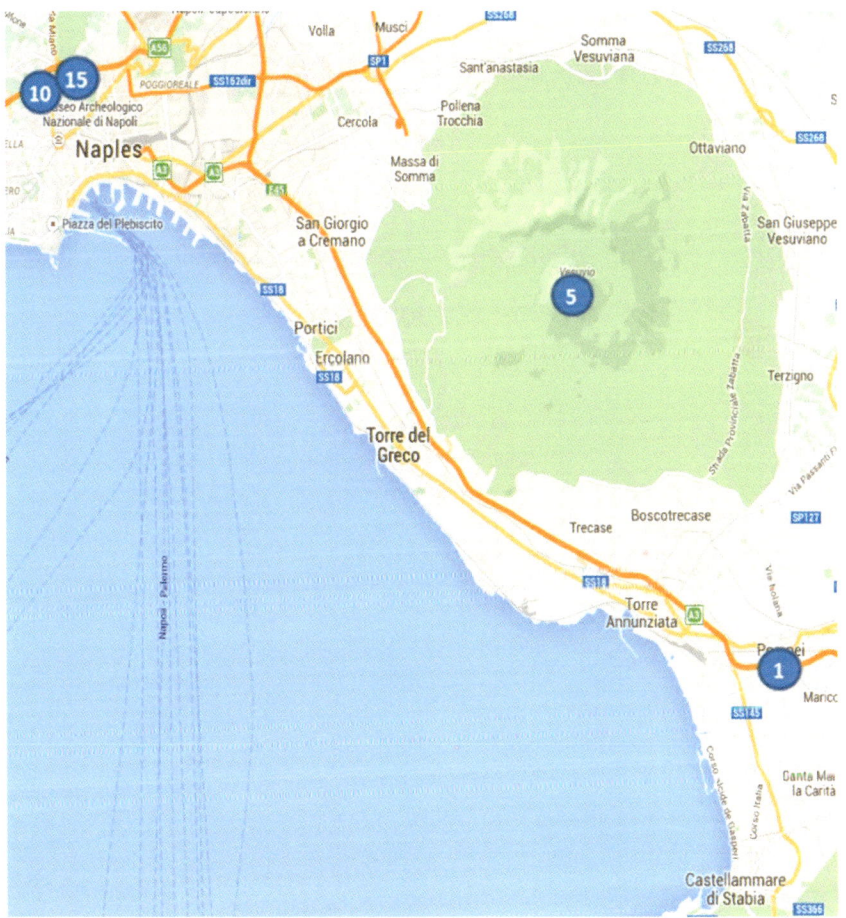

A Note to the Reader

Dear Reader

Thank you for your purchase of this Atsons Travel guide, we hope you have enjoyed reading it!

Please feel free to post an informative, unbiased review on Amazon so that others may benefit from your experience. Reviews help us spread the word of our books and attract fantastic customers such as yourselves.

Also your feedback is invaluable to us, as we work hard to serve you and continually improve our customers' experience.

Sincerely

Atsons Travel Guides